ULTIMATE SPORTS STATS

PRO HOCKEY
BY THE NUMBERS

Percy Leed

Lerner Publications ◆ Minneapolis

Statistics are accurate through the 2022–2023 NHL season.

Copyright © 2025 by Lerner Publishing Group, Inc.

All rights reserved. International copyright secured. No part of this book may be reproduced, stored in a retrieval system, or transmitted in any form or by any means—electronic, mechanical, photocopying, recording, or otherwise—without the prior written permission of Lerner Publishing Group, Inc., except for the inclusion of brief quotations in an acknowledged review.

Lerner Publications Company
An imprint of Lerner Publishing Group, Inc.
241 First Avenue North
Minneapolis, MN 55401 USA

For reading levels and more information, look up this title at www.lernerbooks.com.

Main body text set in Adrianna.
Typeface provided by Chank.

Library of Congress Cataloging-in-Publication Data

Names: Leed, Percy, 1968– author.
Title: Pro hockey by the numbers / Percy Leed.
Description: Minneapolis : Lerner Publications, [2024] | Series: Lerner sports. Ultimate sports stats | "Statistics are through the 2022 National Hockey League regular season unless otherwise noted"—t.p. verso. | Includes bibliographical references and index. | Audience: Ages 7–11 years | Audience: Grades 4–6 | Summary: "Hockey is a fast and exciting sport. Games are full of quick passes, big checks, and thrilling goals. Discover the stats that help fans follow their favorite teams and players"— Provided by publisher.
Identifiers: LCCN 2023048848 (print) | LCCN 2023048849 (ebook) | ISBN 9798765625965 (lib. bdg.) | ISBN 9798765629888 (pbk.) | ISBN 9798765638200 (epub)
Subjects: LCSH: Hockey—Statistics—Juvenile literature. | Hockey—Records—Juvenile literature. | National Hockey League—Juvenile literature.
Classification: LCC GV847.5 .L44 2024 (print) | LCC GV847.5 (ebook) | DDC 796.962/64—dc23/eng/20231128

LC record available at https://lccn.loc.gov/2023048848
LC ebook record available at https://lccn.loc.gov/2023048849

Manufactured in the United States of America
1-1010069-51930-3/6/2024

TABLE OF CONTENTS

INTRODUCTION
THE FIRST GOAL 4

CHAPTER 1
PLAYER STATS 6

CHAPTER 2
TEAM STATS 18

CHAPTER 3
STATS ARE HERE TO STAY 24

    Stats Matchup 28

    Glossary 30

    Learn More. 31

    Index 32

INTRODUCTION
THE FIRST GOAL

The first National Hockey League (NHL) game took place on December 19, 1917. Exactly one minute into the game, Dave Ritchie scored a goal for the Montreal Wanderers. This was the first statistic, or stat, in league history.

Throughout hockey history, fans have used stats to learn more about players and teams. Changes to rules, equipment, and leagues have all had an impact on hockey stats. To understand hockey's important stats, it helps to know about the sport's history.

THE MONTREAL WANDERERS IN 1914

Oh, Canada

The first game of hockey was played in Canada in 1875 with nine players on each side. Teams and leagues soon began to form. In 1909, the National Hockey Association (NHA) started with seven Canadian teams. Eight years later, the NHA became the NHL.

In 1942, the NHL had only six teams. But by the 2022–2023 season, the league had 32 teams. The teams that have existed the longest often have better all-time stats such as total wins and Stanley Cup titles.

A HOCKEY GAME IN FRANCE AROUND 1900

CHAPTER 1
PLAYER STATS

RACKING UP NUMBERS

In the 1944–1945 season, Maurice "Rocket" Richard scored 50 goals in 50 games for the Montreal Canadiens. Wayne Gretzky beat that record in 1981–1982 with 50 goals in just 39 games for the Edmonton Oilers. By the end of the season, Gretzky had scored 92 goals.

MAURICE "ROCKET" RICHARD

MOST GOALS SCORED IN A CAREER

PLAYER	GOALS
Wayne Gretzky	894
Alex Ovechkin	822
Gordie Howe	801
Jaromír Jágr	766
Brett Hull	741

WAYNE GRETZKY

SCORING FRENZY

Joe Malone began playing for the Montreal Canadiens in 1917. Malone scored five goals in his first game. He scored at least one goal in each of his first 14 games! That's still the longest goal-scoring streak to begin a career in NHL history. Malone finished the season with 44 goals and became the league's first single-season scoring leader.

MOST GOALS SCORED IN A SEASON

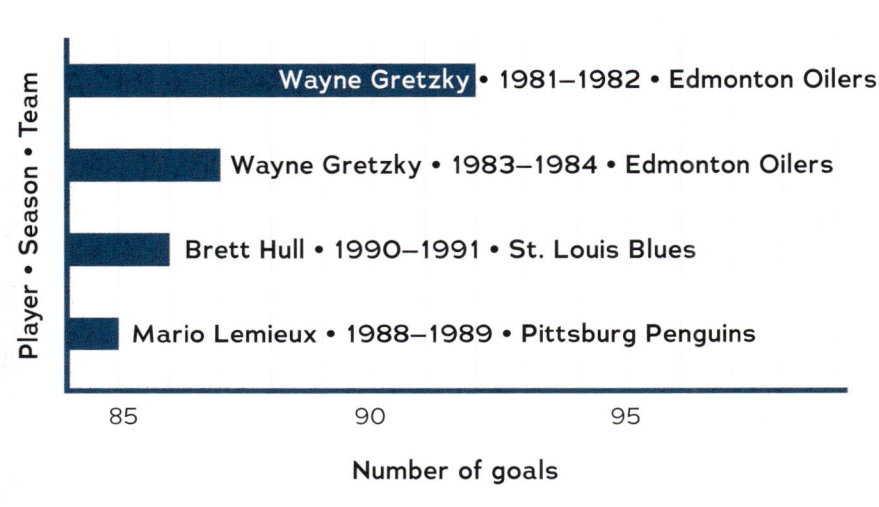

Game-Winning Goals

Some goals are more important than others. For example, the goal that gives a team the lead after a tie is called the go-ahead goal. If no other goals are scored, the go-ahead goal becomes the game-winning goal!

JAROMÍR JÁGR
(*IN RED*)

MOST CAREER GAME-WINNING GOALS

PLAYER	GOALS
Jaromír Jágr	135
Alex Ovechkin	124
Gordie Howe	121
Phil Esposito	118
Brett Hull	110
Teemu Selänne	110

JOE MALONE

HAT TRICK!

One of the most exciting hockey stats is the hat trick. Players achieve a hat trick when they score three goals in one game. The term was inspired by Chicago Black Hawks player Alex Kaleta. Kaleta could not afford to buy a hat in a store. The store owner said Kaleta could have the hat if he scored at least three goals in a game that night. Kaleta scored four goals and got the hat.

MOST CAREER HAT TRICKS	
PLAYER	HAT TRICKS
Wayne Gretzky	50
Mario Lemieux	40
Mike Bossy	39
Brett Hull	33
Phil Esposito	32

WAIT, WHAT!?

Joe Malone is the only player to ever score seven goals in a game. He did it for the Quebec Bulldogs in the 1919–1920 season.

NEED A HAND?

In hockey, the players who pass the puck to a scoring teammate are credited with assists. Assists are given to the last one or two offensive players to shoot, deflect, or just touch the puck before a teammate scores a goal. Wayne Gretzky and Mario Lemieux are two of the NHL's greatest passers.

MARIO LEMIEUX

MOST CAREER ASSISTS PER GAMES PLAYED	
PLAYER	ASSISTS PER GAMES PLAYED
Wayne Gretzky	1.32
Mario Lemieux	1.13
Bobby Orr	0.98
Connor McDavid	0.96
Peter Forsberg	0.90

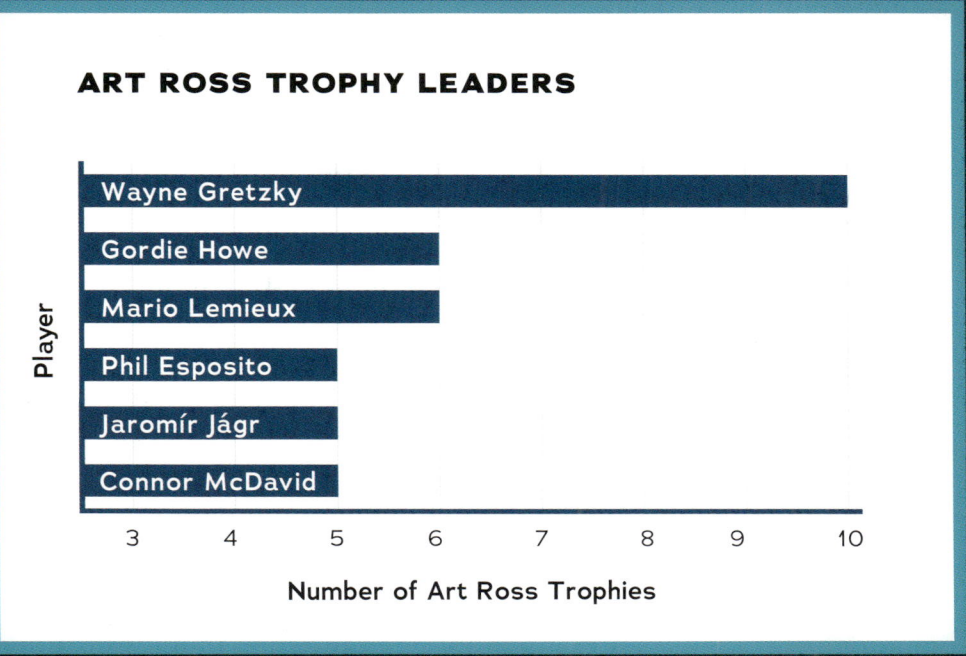

POINTS

A hockey player earns one point for a goal or for an assist. At the end of each season, the NHL points leader receives the Art Ross Trophy. The trophy is named for the former player, coach, and general manager who also designed the NHL puck.

WAIT, WHAT!?

In 2022–2023, Connor McDavid won his fifth Art Ross Trophy in eight seasons in the NHL. Some fans think he'll one day break Gretzky's record of 10 Art Ross Trophies.

TOP OF THEIR GAME

It takes great skill to be ranked among hockey's all-time points leaders. Having a long career also helps. Gordie Howe played in the NHL for 26 seasons. He was 52 years old when he retired. The top five players on the NHL's all-time points list each played for at least 20 seasons.

GORDIE HOWE

ALL-TIME POINTS LEADERS

PLAYER	CAREER	POINTS
Wayne Gretzky	1979–1999	2,857
Jaromír Jágr	1991–2018	1,921
Mark Messier	1979–2004	1,887
Gordie Howe	1946–1980	1,850
Ron Francis	1982–2004	1,798

THE PUCK STOPS HERE

In hockey's early years, goalies were not allowed to drop to the ice to block shots. They didn't even wear helmets or masks! In recent years, goalies use bigger and better equipment. That's one reason why most of the NHL's most successful goalies are from recent seasons.

MARC-ANDRÉ FLEURY

MOST CAREER WINS BY A GOALIE		
PLAYER	CAREER	WINS
Martin Brodeur	1991–2015	691
Patrick Roy	1984–2003	551
Marc-André Fleury	2003–Present	544
Roberto Luongo	1999–2019	489
Ed Belfour	1988–2007	484

SAVED!

Great teams need a great goalie. In a playoff game on March 24, 1936, the Montreal Maroons fired shot after shot at Detroit Red Wings goalie Normie Smith. He faced 92 shots over nine periods and stopped them all. The Red Wings finally scored to win the longest game in NHL history.

ALL-TIME SHUTOUT LEADERS		
PLAYER	CAREER	NUMBER OF SHUTOUTS
Martin Brodeur	1991–2015	125
Terry Sawchuk	1949–1970	103
George Hainsworth	1926–1937	94
Glenn Hall	1952–1971	84
Jacques Plante	1952–1973	82

MARTIN BRODEUR

LINUS ULLMARK

Wait, What!?

In 2022–2023, Boston Bruins goalie Linus Ullmark reached 40 wins after appearing in 49 games. No goalie in NHL history had ever reached 40 wins in a season so quickly.

Breaking the Rules

Referees give players penalties for breaking rules. The player is sent to the penalty box, and their team cannot replace them on the ice. This leaves the team one player short, giving the other team a power play. A minor penalty such as slashing with the stick results in a two-minute power play. A major penalty such as fighting is five minutes.

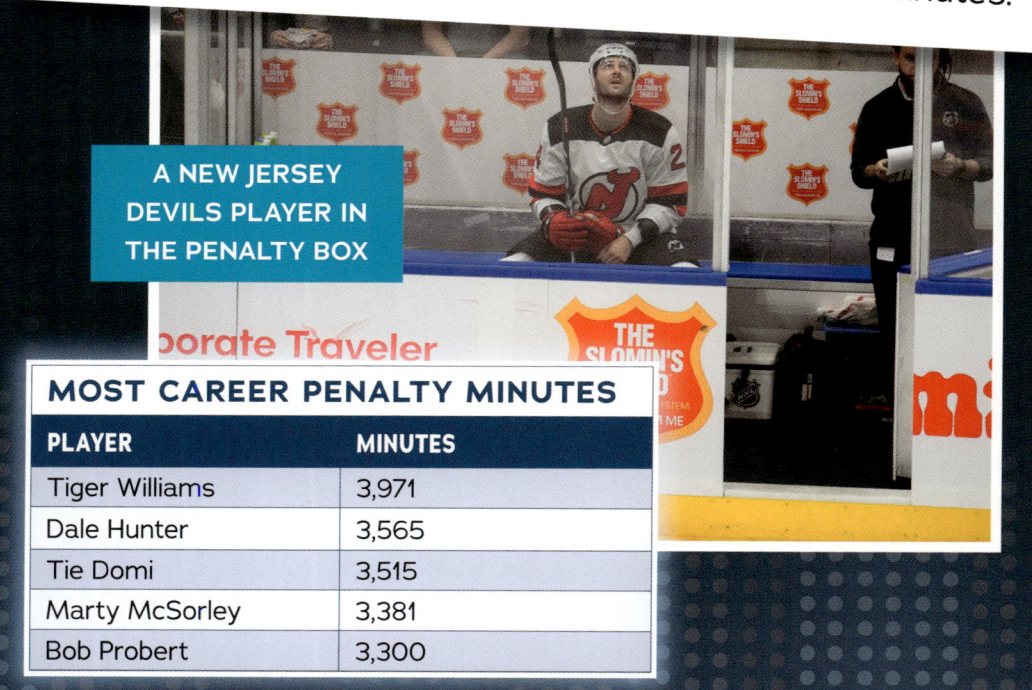

A NEW JERSEY DEVILS PLAYER IN THE PENALTY BOX

MOST CAREER PENALTY MINUTES	
PLAYER	MINUTES
Tiger Williams	3,971
Dale Hunter	3,565
Tie Domi	3,515
Marty McSorley	3,381
Bob Probert	3,300

Wait, What!?

The first NHL player to get more than 300 penalty minutes in a season was Philadelphia Flyers skater Dave Schultz. He had 472 penalty minutes in 1974–1975, which is still the most ever.

The Most Valuable MVP

At the end of each regular season, the Professional Hockey Writers Association votes for the player who is most valuable to their team. The winner receives the Hart Memorial Trophy, the NHL's Most Valuable Player (MVP) award. Wayne Gretzky won the Hart nine times. That's more MVP awards than any other US pro player has won in a team sport.

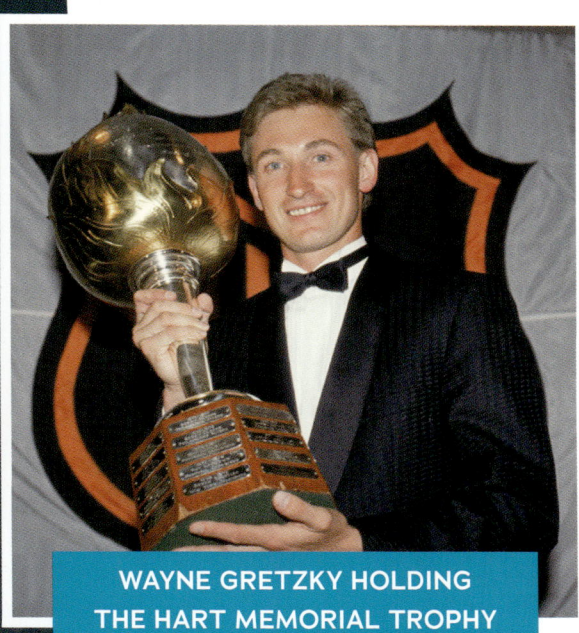

WAYNE GRETZKY HOLDING THE HART MEMORIAL TROPHY

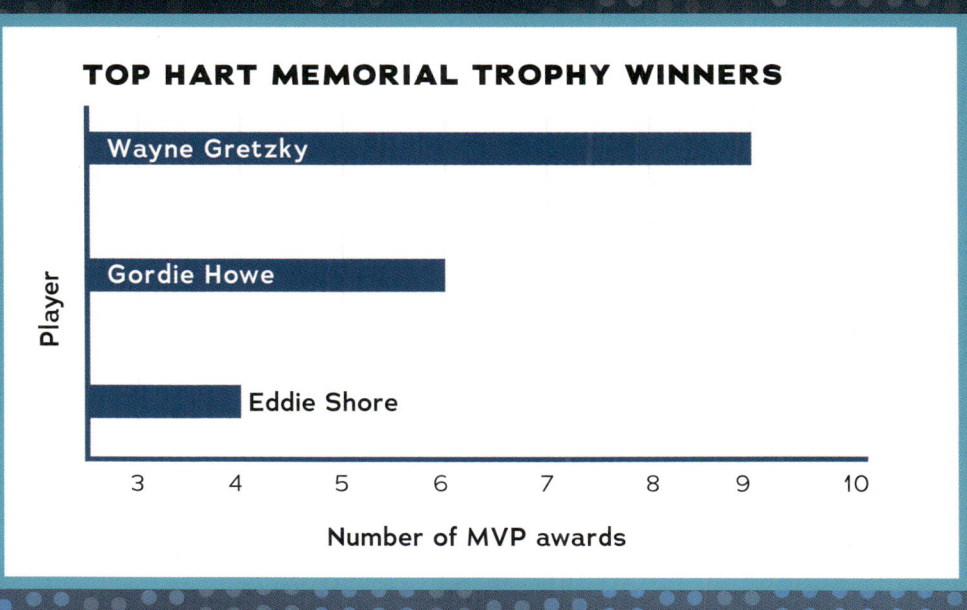

TOP HART MEMORIAL TROPHY WINNERS

CHAPTER 2
TEAM STATS

IT'S ALL ABOUT WINNING

The Presidents' Trophy goes to the NHL team that finishes the regular season with the best record. But having the best regular season record doesn't guarantee playoff success. Since the first Presidents' Trophy in 1985–1986, only seven teams have won it and the Stanley Cup in the same season.

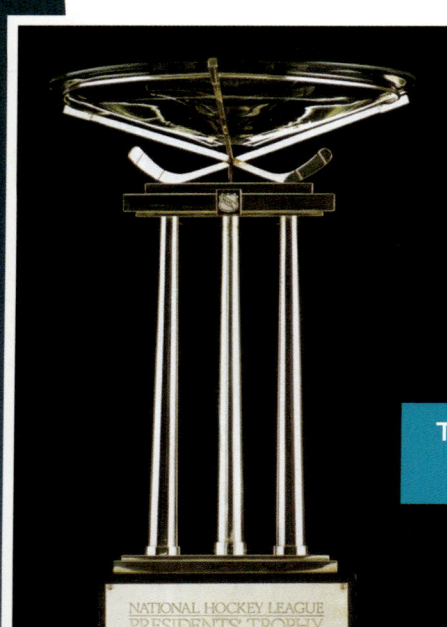

THE PRESIDENTS' TROPHY

MOST PRESIDENTS' TROPHIES	
TEAM	PRESIDENTS' TROPHIES
Detroit Red Wings	6
Boston Bruins	4
Colorado Avalanche	3
New York Rangers	3
Washington Capitals	3

STEADY WINNERS

The Minnesota Wild were a new team in 2000–2001. In their first 15 seasons, the Wild made the playoffs seven times. That's not bad for a new team! The Detroit Red Wings date back to the 1920s. In 2015–2016, the Red Wings made the playoffs for the 25th year in a row. Their streak ended the next season.

DETROIT RED WINGS PLAYERS IN 2016

TEAMS WITH THE MOST PLAYOFF APPEARANCES

TEAM	NUMBER OF PLAYOFF APPEARANCES
Montreal Canadiens	85
Boston Bruins	76
Toronto Maple Leafs	72
Detroit Red Wings	64
Chicago Blackhawks	63

WINNING THE CUP

The goal of every NHL player is to win the Stanley Cup. The trophy is named after former Canadian governor general Frederick Arthur Stanley. He awarded the first cup to the Montreal Amateur Athletic Association in 1893. Each year the names of the winning team's players, coaches, and staff are added to the base of the cup.

THE MONTREAL AMATEUR ATHLETIC ASSOCIATION WITH THE STANLEY CUP

PITTSBURGH PENGUINS STAR MARIO LEMIEUX

MOST STANLEY CUPS SINCE 1926–1927

Team

- Montreal Canadiens
- Toronto Maple Leafs
- Detroit Red Wings
- Boston Bruins
- Chicago Blackhawks
- Edmonton Oilers
- Pittsburgh Penguins

5 6 7 8 9 10 11 12 13 14 15 16 17 18 19 20 21 22 23

Number of Stanley Cups

STREAK!

Sometimes a team goes on a streak and wins game after game. But streaks go both ways. Some teams can't seem to win against any opponent.

1975–1976   In their first season (1974–1975), the Washington Capitals finished with an 8–67–5 record, the worst NHL record of all time. Their second season wasn't much better. They won 11 games. But they also went 25 games in a row without a win.

1977–1978   The Montreal Canadiens went on a 28-game undefeated streak on their way to winning the cup. They won the Stanley Cup six times in the 1970s.

1979–1980   The Philadelphia Flyers were a team of tough players known as the Broad Street Bullies. Seven Flyers each racked up more than 100 minutes of penalties for the season. Despite so much time in the penalty box, the team went on a record-breaking 35-game winning streak.

1980–1981   The Winnipeg Jets finished the season 9–57–14. Their terrible record included a 30-game losing streak.

1992–1993   The Pittsburgh Penguins were on their way to a third straight Stanley Cup title with 17 straight victories and the Presidents' Trophy. But they lost in the second round of the playoffs.

2022–2023   In their first six games, the New Jersey Devils were 3–3. Then they had an epic winning streak. They won 13 games in a row and tied for the fifth longest streak in NHL history.

LIGHTING THE LAMP

When a goal is scored, a red light behind the net turns on. Fans call this lighting the lamp. In the 1981–1982 season, the Edmonton Oilers became the first NHL team to score over 400 goals in a season. That's a lot of lamp lighting!

THE GOAL LIGHT COMES ON TO SIGNAL A GOAL.

MOST GOALS SCORED IN A SEASON		
SEASON	TEAM	GOALS SCORED
1983–1984	Edmonton Oilers	446
1985–1986	Edmonton Oilers	426
1982–1983	Edmonton Oilers	424
1981–1982	Edmonton Oilers	417
1984–1985	Edmonton Oilers	401

CHAPTER 3
STATS ARE HERE TO STAY

GAME SUMMARIES

One way to compare player and team stats is by looking at a line score. A line score shows the final score of a game. It also shows who scored. Use the key on the next page to understand the line score from the last game of the 2022–2023 Stanley Cup Final.

ALEC MARTINEZ

KEY

1 =	first period
2 =	second period
3 =	third period
T =	total goals

FINAL SCORING SUMMARY (LINE SCORE)

FINAL	1	2	3	T
Florida Panthers	0	1	2	3
Vegas Golden Knights	2	4	3	9

SCORING SUMMARY

FIRST PERIOD
SCORING
- 11:52 – Knights Mark Stone
- 13:41 – Knights Nicolas Hague

SECOND PERIOD
SCORING
- 2:15 – Panthers Aaron Ekblad
- 10:28 – Knights Alec Martinez
- 12:13 – Knights Reilly Smith
- 17:15 – Knights Mark Stone
- 19:58 – Knights Michael Amadio

THIRD PERIOD
SCORING
- 8:22 – Knights Ivan Barbashev
- 8:47 – Panthers Sam Reinhart
- 11:39 – Panthers Sam Bennett
- 14:06 – Knights Mark Stone
- 18:58 – Knights Nicolas Roy

NICOLAS ROY WITH THE STANLEY CUP

A PLAYER WITH GREAT STATS IS MORE LIKELY TO BE CHOSEN BY A TEAM DURING THE NHL DRAFT.

Game Action

Fans love to study stats to compare players and teams. Players, coaches, and agents use stats too. Stats help teams decide which new players to draft and how much money to pay them.

Coaches also use stats to decide who will play certain games. For example, goalies who play two nights in a row usually don't play as well on the second night. The coach may decide to play the backup goalie more often.

Fantasy and the Future

Some adult fans want to get even more involved with the stats of their favorite players and teams. In fantasy hockey leagues, fans draft players to form teams. Fantasy teams earn points based on the real stats of NHL players.

NHL teams hire people to study stats. These experts help players and teams come up with new ways to play. High-tech devices in players' jerseys and pucks track skating and shooting speeds. These stats help players and fans understand the game.

AN ANAHEIM DUCKS COACH (*CENTER*) TALKS WITH TWO PLAYERS DURING A GAME.

STATS MATCHUP

Connor McDavid and Nathan MacKinnon are both forwards at the top of their game. McDavid has won the Art Ross Trophy five times and the Hart Memorial trophy three times. MacKinnon has been one of the top 10 scorers in the league for four seasons straight. Of the two, McDavid is the only one to win the Art Ross and Hart Memorial trophies. But MacKinnon has won the Stanley Cup.

CONNOR MCDAVID EDMONTON OILERS	
Games played	569
Shots	1,948
Goals	303
Assists	547
Points	850
Game-winning goals	64
MVPs	3
Stanley Cup titles	0

CONNOR MCDAVID

Here are their career stats through the 2022–2023 regular season. Who is the stronger forward? You decide.

NATHAN MACKINNON COLORADO AVALANCHE	
Games played	709
Shots	2,767
Goals	284
Assists	475
Points	759
Game-winning goals	55
MVPs	0
Stanley Cup titles	1

NATHAN MACKINNON

Glossary

agent: a person who represents players, mainly for matters involving money

assist: a pass from a teammate that leads directly to a goal

deflect: to redirect a shot

hat trick: three goals scored by one player in a game

period: one of the divisions of playing time in a game. Hockey has three periods.

regular season: when all of the teams in a league play one another to determine playoff teams

save: when a goalkeeper prevents shots on goal from crossing the goal line

shutout: a game in which one team does not score any goals

winning streak: a period or series of wins

Learn More

Anderson, Josh. *Sidney Crosby vs. Wayne Gretzky: Who Would Win?* Minneapolis: Lerner Publications, 2024.

Britannica Kids: Ice Hockey
https://kids.britannica.com/kids/article/Ice-Hockey/353257

Ducksters: Hockey
https://www.ducksters.com/sports/hockey.php

Graves, Will. *Colorado Avalanche*. Mendota Heights, MN: Press Box Books, 2023.

National Hockey League Facts for Kids
https://kids.kiddle.co/National_Hockey_League

Walker, Tracy Sue. *Wayne Gretzky: The Great One*. Minneapolis: Lerner Publications, 2023.

INDEX

fantasy hockey, 27

goalie, 13–15, 26

Gretzky, Wayne, 6–7, 9–12, 17

hat trick, 9

Lemieux, Mario, 7, 9–11

National Hockey Association, 5

penalty, 16, 22

playoffs, 14, 18–19, 22

Presidents' Trophy, 18, 22

Stanley Cup, 5, 18, 20–22, 24

PHOTO ACKNOWLEDGMENTS

Image credits: B Bennett/Getty Images, pp. 4, 9, 17, 20; Roger Viollet Collection/Getty Images, p. 5; Robert Riger/Getty Images, p. 6; Bruce Bennett/Getty Images, p. 7; Andy Marlin/Getty Images, p. 8; Rick Stewart/Stringer/Getty Images, p. 10; Bettmann/Getty Images, p. 12; Norm Hall/Getty Images, p. 13; Christopher Pasatieri/Getty Images, p. 14; Icon Sportswire/Getty Images, pp. 15–16; Silvia Pecota/StringerGetty Images, p. 18; Christian Petersen/Getty Images, p. 19; Mike Ehrmann/Getty Images, p. 21; AP Photo/Winslow Townson, p. 23; Patrick Smith/Getty Images, p. 24; Ethan Miller/Getty Images, p. 25; AP Photo/George Walker IV, p. 26; Debora Robinson/Getty Images, p. 27; Andy Devlin/Getty Images, p. 28; Minas Panagiotakis/Getty Images, p. 29.

Design elements: Ali Kahfi/Getty Images; sarayut Thaneerat/Getty Images.

Cover: AP Photo/Mark Zaleski.